The Best Wedding Gift

Written by
Cath Jones

Illustrated by
Pauline Reeves

In a week, Jill will go to a wedding.

It will be her mums' wedding.

But Jill needs to get them
a wedding gift.

Jill set off with her gran on a trip to the shops.

"Have you got some gifts that my mums will like?" she said.

But shopping was hard.
Things cost so much.

Did Jill get a good wedding gift?

No, she did not get a gift at all.

Jill was a bit sad.

Jill and her mums set off to the wedding.

Mum was in green satin and Mom was in red velvet.

"You look fab!" Jill said.

In the park was a big oak tree. This was such a good spot for the wedding.

They all stood under the tree.

It did rain a bit – but not too much.

Mom and Mum said vows.

Jill had a card for her mums
and she sang them a song.

She was still a bit sad
that she had no gift for them.

But her mums said, "No need to fret, Jill! We do not need a wedding gift from you."

"A card and a song are fab wedding gifts from you," they said. "And a big wedding hug!"

"My mums' wedding was the best ever!" Jill said.